A New True Book

THE NETHERLANDS

By Karen Jacobsen

Flag of the Netherlands

CHILDRENS PRESS®
CHICAGO

Wind-powered generators have replaced some of the windmills in the Netherlands.

Project Editor: Fran Dyra
Design: Margrit Fiddle

Library of Congress Cataloging-in-Publication Data

Jacobsen, Karen.
 The Netherlands / by Karen Jacobsen.
  p.   cm. — (A New true book)
 Includes index.
 Summary: An introduction to a country with half its land at or below sea level, whose name literally means lowlands.
  ISBN 0-516-01137-5
  1. Netherlands—Juvenile literature.
[1. Netherlands.] I. Title.
DJ18.J34 1992
949.2—dc20   91-37974
                                                CIP
                                                 AC

PHOTO CREDITS

AP/Wide World Photos, Inc.—30, 32

Reprinted with permission of *The New Book of Knowledge*, 1990 edition, © Grolier Inc.—5

H. Armstrong Roberts, Inc.—© M. Thonig, 14 (top)

Historical Pictures Service/Chicago—19 (2 photos), 21, 24, 25, 27 (top and bottom left, center)

© Joan Kalbacken—15, 40 (2 photos), 41, 42

© Emilie Lepthien—36

Photri—© Jack Novak, 39

© Porterfield/Chickering—35 (left), 43 (left)

© Ann Purcell—17 (right), 18 (right)

© Carl Purcell—16 (2 photos), 18 (left)

The Royal Netherlands Embassy, Washington, D.C.—7, 10

SuperStock International, Inc.—8, 14 (bottom), 23, 34, 37 (2 photos); © Eric Carle, 12; © Metropolitan Museum of Art, N.Y.C., 27 (right); © David Warren, 31 (left); © Oliver Troisfontaines, 44 (right)

TSW-CLICK/Chicago—2; © Tony Craddock, Cover; © Glen Allison, 6 (right); © David Hanson, 6 (left), 31 (right), 44 (left); © Doris De Witt, 9; © Dan Sweeney, 29; © E. N. Van Loo, 43 (right); © Manfred Mehlig, 45

Valan—© T. Joyce, Cover inset, 35 (right); © Arthur Strange, 17 (left)

Cover—Holland, near Alkmaar, windmill, sheep grazing

Cover Inset—Old canal, side houses

TABLE OF CONTENTS

THE NATION

The Netherlands is in Europe on the coast of the North Sea. Two nations share borders with the Netherlands–Germany in the east and Belgium in the south.

The Netherlands has twelve provinces, including North Holland and South Holland. Sometimes people use "Holland" as another name for the Netherlands.

More than 14.5 million

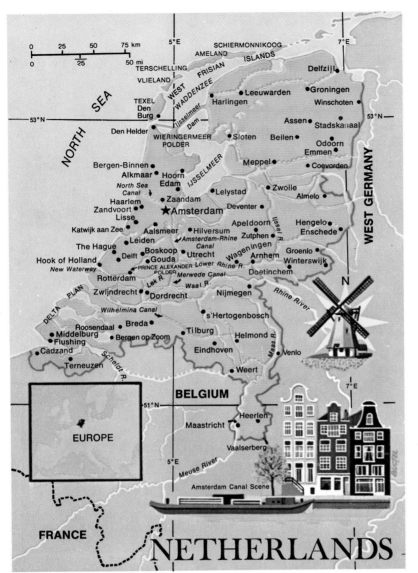

From north to south, the Netherlands measures only about 200 miles. At its widest, it is less than 170 miles across.

people live in this small country. They speak Dutch. The Dutch word for Netherlands

5

A busy street in Amsterdam, the capital city of the Netherlands (left). Millions of flowers (right) are grown in the Netherlands and sold throughout the world.

is *Nederlanden,* which means "lowlands." This is a perfect name for the nation because half of its land lies at sea level or lower. The North Sea beats against the nation's

6

Seawater rushes through a broken dike near Terneuzen, flooding the polders.

coastline. Many times, the sea's rough waters have rushed inland, causing many deaths and great damage.

Two major European rivers—the Rhine and the Maas—pass through the

Netherlands on their way to the North Sea. Some of the nation's other rivers are the Amstel, the Waal, the Lek, and the IJssel. A system of canals connects the rivers and carries boat traffic throughout the nation.

Canals like this one in Marken are important means of transportation.

Government buildings in The Hague

The Netherlands is a democracy. It has a constitution and a parliament. It also has a queen and a royal family. Amsterdam is the nation's capital city. The parliament meets in a city named The Hague.

A system of windmills is used to drain water from the land.
This group is in the province of South Holland.

THE LAND

Much of the Netherlands was once covered by shallow water. For hundreds of years, the hardworking Netherlanders have "made" dry land by building *polders.*

To make a polder, a strong dam, called a dike, is built all around a wet area. Then the water is pumped into canals that flow into the North Sea.

About two-fifths of the

Houses are built along the canals

Netherlands is polder land. Farms and cities are built on polders. The Prins Alexander Polder, the lowest land in the Netherlands, is 22 feet below sea level.

Miles of sand dunes–
built up by the wind–line
the nation's seacoast. The
dunes help protect the
polder lands against
flooding from the sea.

The eastern part of the
Netherlands is called the
Sand Plains. This region
rises as much as 100 feet
above sea level. The land
is sandy, with many small
forests of beech, oak, and
pine trees. Without irrigation,
the soil is too dry for raising

Cattle grazing on polder land (above), and farmers (below)
harvesting crops in the southern part of the Netherlands

Sheep grazing on the polders

crops. Cattle, sheep, and horses graze on pastures in the Sand Plains.

The Uplands are hills and ridges in the far southeastern part of the Netherlands. Here, the nation's highest point, the Vaalser Berg, rises 1,057 feet. Fruit and vegetable crops grow in the Uplands.

THE PEOPLE

Thousands of years ago, several tribes from what is now central Europe settled along the seacoast. Each tribe had its own language and customs. Most

Most Netherlanders are descended from ancient European tribes.

Children (left) fishing in a canal at Amsterdam. A young woman (right) eats raw herring in the traditional Dutch way.

Netherlanders are descendants of these early people.

Today, people from many other lands live in the Netherlands. Many thousands came from Indonesia in Asia and from

17

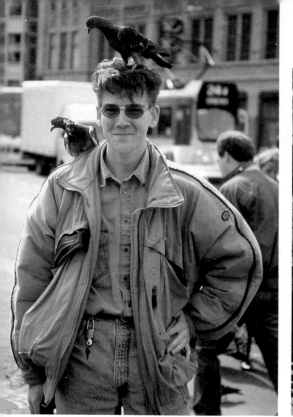

Surinam in South America—
former colonies of the
Netherlands. Thousands
more came from Turkey,
Morocco, and several
southern European nations
to work in the Netherlands.

Julius Caesar (left) led the Romans into the Netherlands. The drawing (right) shows Roman building projects in the Low Countries—the Netherlands, Belgium, and Luxembourg.

LONG AGO IN THE NETHERLANDS

In 58 B.C., Julius Caesar led a Roman army into the lowlands. The Romans took over. They built trading centers, roads, and dikes. For more than four hundred years, the Netherlands, Belgium, and Luxembourg were part of the Roman Empire. They were called the Low Countries.

After the Romans, tribes from other parts of Europe took over. In the A.D. 700s, the Franks, a Germanic tribe, came to power. They ruled over the Low Countries and most of western Europe. Charlemagne (742-814) was their emperor.

Charlemagne brought law and order to his empire.

After Charlemagne, the European empire of the Franks was divided into three kingdoms. The Netherlands were part of the middle kingdom, which stretched across Europe from Italy to the North Sea.

DANGERS FROM THE SEA

Life along the North Sea was dangerous. Storms caused floods that killed people and ruined crops. Vikings from Norway and Denmark attacked lowland villages.

To stop the Vikings, the king chose local leaders to defend parts of the kingdom. The leaders, called counts, led armies and built castles and fortresses. They stopped the raiders.

Towns grew up around the safety of castle walls.

The people of the
Netherlands needed more
land to live on. In the
1100s they built more
dikes and polders.
Amsterdam, The Hague,
and Rotterdam began as
small settlements on
polders in the 1200s.

PHILIP II OF SPAIN

Philip II of Spain was the son of Emperor Charles V.

In 1555, Philip II became the king of Spain. He also ruled the Low Countries and other parts of Europe. Philip and most of the people under his rule were Roman Catholics. But many people in the Low Countries were Protestants. Philip sent a Spanish army to force all the lowlanders to become Catholics.

WILLIAM THE SILENT

William I was called William the Silent because he thought before speaking. He also was called the "Father of the Netherlands."

In 1568 William I, the prince of Orange and a Protestant, led a revolt against Philip's army. In William's army there were both Protestants and Catholics. Together, they fought the Spanish.

In 1581, William and the seven northern provinces (the Netherlands) declared themselves a free country. **25**

THE GOLDEN AGE

In the 1600s the Netherlands grew powerful. Its ships sailed to every corner of the world. Its merchants started colonies in faraway lands.

At home, the skillful Netherlanders led the world in shipbuilding, mapmaking, printing, and other trades. Their merchants set up banks and made fortunes by lending money.

Desiderius Erasmus (top left) and Christiaan Huygens (bottom left) were two great Dutch scholars. Vincent Van Gogh (center) and Rembrandt Van Rijn (right) were two of the greatest painters in history.

The wealth of the Netherlands also supported the arts, especially painting, and science. The ideas and discoveries of scholars in their universities changed the world.

27

WAR AND PEACE

From the 1600s to the 1800s, the Netherlands was often at war with England or France. Each nation wanted to rule on land and sea. The cost of these wars–in lives and property–weakened the Netherlands. From 1795 to 1813, France ruled the Netherlands.

By the middle of the 1800s, Netherlanders were busy making improvements instead of war. New canals linked Amsterdam and

The Zuider Zee dike created several huge polders and a lake called the IJssel Meer.

Rotterdam to the North Sea. New factories made cloth, steel, chemicals, and other products. New tools and methods helped farmers reap huge harvests. Crops were sold around the world. When World War I began in 1914, the Netherlands did not take part.

WORLD WAR II

In May 1940, German airplanes bombed the Netherlands. The port city of Rotterdam was almost destroyed. The German army marched in and took over the country for five years.

Rotterdam was heavily damaged by German bombers. More than 300,000 people were killed during World War II.

After World War II, the
city of Rotterdam was rebuilt
with new, modern houses.

After the defeat of
Germany in 1945, the
Netherlanders began to
rebuild their country. They
repaired polders, canals,
and dikes. They built new
factories and new farms.
They worked hard and
were very successful.

In 1953, floodwaters killed 1,858 people.
The floods destroyed 35,000 cattle and a million acres of farmland.

TODAY IN THE NETHERLANDS

The people of the Netherlands must always be on guard against the sea. In 1953, a terrible flood killed 1,858 people.

Since then, the Netherlanders have built huge dikes across the mouths of several of their southern rivers.

In 1932 a dike was built across the mouth of the Zuider Zee. Today, one part of the former sea is now a huge polder, and the rest is a freshwater lake called IJssel Meer.

There are more than 1,000 people for every square mile of land in the Netherlands. Many people

Amsterdam is a beautiful city full of old-fashioned houses and winding canals.

live in country villages, but most Netherlanders live in cities.

Since the 1600s, the Netherlands has been known for its crafts. Today's Netherlanders produce beautiful ceramics and fabrics, as well as

Hand-painted blue-and-white Delft ware (left) is a famous product of Dutch craft workers. The Netherlands is also known for its many fine cheeses.

glass, gold, and silver wares. Also, Amsterdam is a world center for the cutting of diamonds.

Dutch cheeses and flowers are sold throughout the world.

Netherlanders enjoy some of the world's

Visitors enjoy *rijsttaffel* in an Amsterdam restaurant.

tastiest food. *Rijsttaffel*
(rice table) is a huge feast
of Indonesian origin. Its
many dishes are made of
spices, fruits, meats, fish,
and a variety of vegetables.

The Netherlands is a
modern nation. Yet some
village people still live as

their ancestors did long ago. Many wear *klompen,* wooden shoes that stay dry—even in the Netherlands' damp climate. Each village has its own special styles of clothing.

Left: Making *klompen.* These wooden shoes are worn with heavy socks for comfort. Right: This woman wears *klompen* with the special costume of her village.

HOLIDAYS

Important holidays for Netherlanders are the Queen's Birthday (April 30), Liberation Day (May 5, celebrating the end of World War II), and the opening of parliament (third Tuesday in September).

Most Netherlanders also celebrate Easter and Christmas. Gifts are exchanged on St. Nicholas' Eve (December 5).

38

These children stop for a snack on the way home from school.

EDUCATION

The government supports both public and private schools. All children from age 6 to 16 must go to school. Primary schools have six grades. Students

A Dutch elementary school (left) and a high-school home economics class

study language arts, arithmetic, and sciences.

There are different kinds of high schools. Some students take the general course, which includes English or other foreign languages. They graduate

at age 18 prepared for
jobs in business.

Vocational schools train
students to be skilled
workers. On-the-job
apprentice programs start
at age 16.

Students learn bricklaying at a vocational school in Groningen.

An old church is now the home of the University of Amsterdam.

The best students take the pre-university course. These graduates must pass a hard test to enter one of the Netherlands' fine universities. The oldest, at Leiden, was founded by William I in 1575.

SPORTS

Football (soccer) is a national pastime for Netherlanders. Bicycle races and yachting events are also popular. Winter sports include ice-skating and iceboating.

Cycling and ice-skating are two popular pastimes in the Netherlands.

Today's Netherlanders
enjoy a high standard of
living. The Netherlands is
a world leader in
manufacturing, and ranks

The World Trade Centre in Amsterdam (inset)
and the Keukenhof Gardens

as Europe's busiest
shipping center. Its
products reach markets in
every corner of the world.
Tourists come from around
the world to enjoy the
beauty and the comforts of
life in the Netherlands.

WORDS YOU SHOULD KNOW

apprentice (uh • PREN • tiss) — a person who learns a trade by helping someone who is skilled in that trade

canal (kuh • NAL) — a waterway dug across land

ceramics (sir • AM • iks) — objects such as dishes and vases made from hardened and painted clay

colony (KAHL • uh • nee) — a settlement of people from another country

constitution (kahn • stih • TOO • shun) — a set of rules or laws for the government of a group of people

continent (KAHN • tih • nent) — a large landmass on the earth

customs (KUSS • tumz) — usual ways of doing things

democracy (dih • MAH • kra • see) — rule by the people or by representatives of the people

descendant (dih • SEN • dint) — a child or a grandchild; a person who comes later in a family line

empire (EM • pyre) — a number of countries under the same government

fortress (FOR • triss) — a building with strong walls for defense against an enemy

irrigation (eer • ih • GAY • shun) — the bringing of water to croplands by building canals, or artificial channels

klompen (KLAHMP • in) — wooden shoes

merchants (MER • chintz) — people who buy and sell products

parliament (PARL • uh • mint) — the lawmaking body of some governments

pasture (PASS • cher) — grasslands where animals such as sheep and cattle graze

polder (POLE • der) — dry land that once was covered by shallow water

province (PRAH • vince) — a division of a country, like a state of the United States

rijsttaffel (RICE • tah • fil) — "rice table"; a feast of many different dishes

tribe (TRYB) — a group of people related by blood and customs

university (yoo • nih • VER • sih • tee) — a school of higher learning

yachting (YAW • ting) — racing or cruising in sailboats

INDEX

About the Author

Karen Jacobsen is a graduate of the University of Connecticut and Syracuse University. She has been a teacher and is a writer. She likes to find out about interesting subjects and then write about them.